SPOT-THE-DIFFERENCES
ACROSS THE USA

TONY J. TALLARICO

DOVER PUBLICATIONS, INC.
MINEOLA, NEW YORK

Planet Friendly Publishing
✔ Made in the United States
✔ Printed on Recycled Paper
Learn more at www.greenedition.org

At Dover Publications we're committed to producing books in an earth-friendly manner and to helping our customers make greener choices.

Manufacturing books in the United States ensures compliance with strict environmental laws and eliminates the need for international freight shipping, a major contributor to global air pollution.

And printing on recycled paper helps minimize our consumption of trees, water and fossil fuels. The text of *Spot-the-Differences Across the USA* was printed on paper made with 30% post-consumer waste, and the cover was printed on paper made with 10% post-consumer waste. According to Environmental Defense's Paper Calculator, by using this innovative paper instead of conventional papers, we achieved the following environmental benefits:

Trees Saved: 8 • Air Emissions Eliminated: 702 pounds
Water Saved: 2,877 gallons • Solid Waste Eliminated: 374 pounds

For more information on our environmental practices, please visit us online at www.doverpublications.com/green

Bibliographical Note

Spot-the-Differences Across the USA is a new work, first published by Dover Publications, Inc., in 2008.

International Standard Book Number

ISBN-13: 978-0-486-46827-3
ISBN-10: 0-486-46827-5

Manufactured in the United States of America
Dover Publications, Inc., 31 East 2nd Street, Mineola, N.Y. 11501

Publisher's Note

This fun-filled book will take you all over the U.S.A. as you learn about important national monuments and parks, famous buildings, and other well-known parts of American history. Each activity consists of two pictures facing each other. On the left is the original picture, and opposite it on the right is a similar picture—except for the fact that fifteen things in the original picture are different! Look carefully at both pictures and spot the fifteen differences as you go along. For example, in the first pair of pictures, pages 4 and 5, you'll see the Capitol building. There is a lamppost in the lower right corner of the right-hand picture. That lamppost does not appear in the left-hand picture, so draw a circle around it on page 5. When you have spotted and circled fifteen items on a page, you're ready to move on to the next set of pictures. There's a Solutions section beginning on page 44, if you want to check your work.

Now, get ready to learn some fascinating facts about American history, such as the names of the presidents shown on Mount Rushmore, the height of Seattle's Space Needle, and the location of the Gateway Arch. Good luck!

The United States Capitol building is located in Washington, D.C., on top of Capitol Hill. It houses the meeting chambers of the House of Representatives and the Senate.

Spot and circle
15 things
that are different
between these
two pictures of the
Capitol building.

Devils Tower is a national monument in Wyoming, near the Black Hills of South Dakota. Meaning "Bear Lodge," it is a volcanic landform that rises 1,267 feet into the air.

Spot and circle
15 things that
are different
between these
two pictures of
Devils Tower.

Everglades National Park in South Florida is the largest subtropical wilderness area in the U.S. Dedicated as a national park in 1947, Everglades is a haven for wildlife, offering visitors campgrounds and hiking trails.

Spot and circle 15 things that are
different between these two pictures
of Everglades National Park.

The Gateway Arch, on the bank of the Mississippi River in St. Louis, Missouri, attracts about one million visitors a year. At 630 feet high, it is the tallest national monument in the U.S.

Spot and circle
15 things that are different between these
two pictures of the Gateway Arch.

The Golden Gate Bridge, in California, connects the city of San Francisco to Marin County. When completed in 1937, the Golden Gate became the longest suspension bridge in the world.

Spot and circle
15 things that are different
between these two pictures of
the Golden Gate Bridge.

Graceland is the 13.8-acre estate that once belonged to
Elvis Presley, the "king of rock and roll." Located in Memphis,
Tennessee, it is now a museum and
a National Historic Landmark.

Spot and circle
15 things that are different between
these two pictures of Graceland.

An awesome, inspiring landscape, the Gra[...]
located in Arizona. It was carved out by the Colo[...]
River over many millions of years!

Spot and circle
15 things that are different between these
two pictures of the Grand Canyon.

The Hollywood Sign is a famous landmark located in the
Hollywood Hills of Los Angeles, California. Originally created
as an advertisement in 1923, its letters stand fifty feet tall!

Spot and circle
15 things that are different between these
two pictures of the Hollywood Sign.

The Hoover Dam is a 726.4-foot-high concrete dam in the Black Canyon of the Colorado River (between Arizona and Nevada). The dam generates enough electricity a year to serve approximately 1.3 million people!

Spot and circle
15 things that are different between these
two pictures of the Hoover Dam.

Located on Chestnut Street in
Philadelphia, Pennsylvania,
Independence Hall is the place
where the Declaration of
Independence was adopted.

Spot and circle
15 things that are different
between these two pictures
of Independence Hall.

The Kennedy Space Center Visitor Complex in Florida is home to museums, theaters, and numerous tours. It is part of the John F. Kennedy Space Center—NASA's launch headquarters.

Spot and circle
15 things that are different
between these two pictures
of the Kennedy Space Center
Visitor Complex.

Monticello was the estate of Thomas Jefferson, the third U.S. president and author of the Declaration of Independence. Jefferson himself designed the 43-room house, located in Virginia.

Spot and circle
15 things that are different
between these
two pictures of Monticello.

South Dakota's Mount Rushmore
National Memorial is a granite sculpture
of four U.S. presidents. The 60-foot-tall
stone faces depict George Washington,
Thomas Jefferson, Theodore Roosevelt,
and Abraham Lincoln.

Spot and circle
15 things that are
different between these
two pictures of
Mount Rushmore.

Niagara Falls is a set of gigantic
waterfalls located on the
Niagara River, which flows along
the border of New York and
Ontario, Canada.

Spot and circle
15 things that are
different between these
two pictures of
Niagara Falls.

Old Faithful, a geyser located
in Yellowstone National Park,
may be the most-photographed
geyser in the world. Eruptions
of boiling water can reach from
106 to 184 feet high!

Spot and circle
15 things that are
different between these
two pictures of
Old Faithful.

Built in 1723, the Old North Church is located on Salem Street in Boston, Massachusetts. It is the place where the famous "One if by land, and two if by sea" lantern signal was sent to Paul Revere and other revolutionaries on the night of April 18, 1775.

Spot and circle
15 things that are
different between these
two pictures of the
Old North Church.

The Sears Tower, in Chicago, Illinois, is the tallest building in the U.S. Originally commissioned by Sears, Roebuck and Company in 1970, this skyscraper has 110 floors.

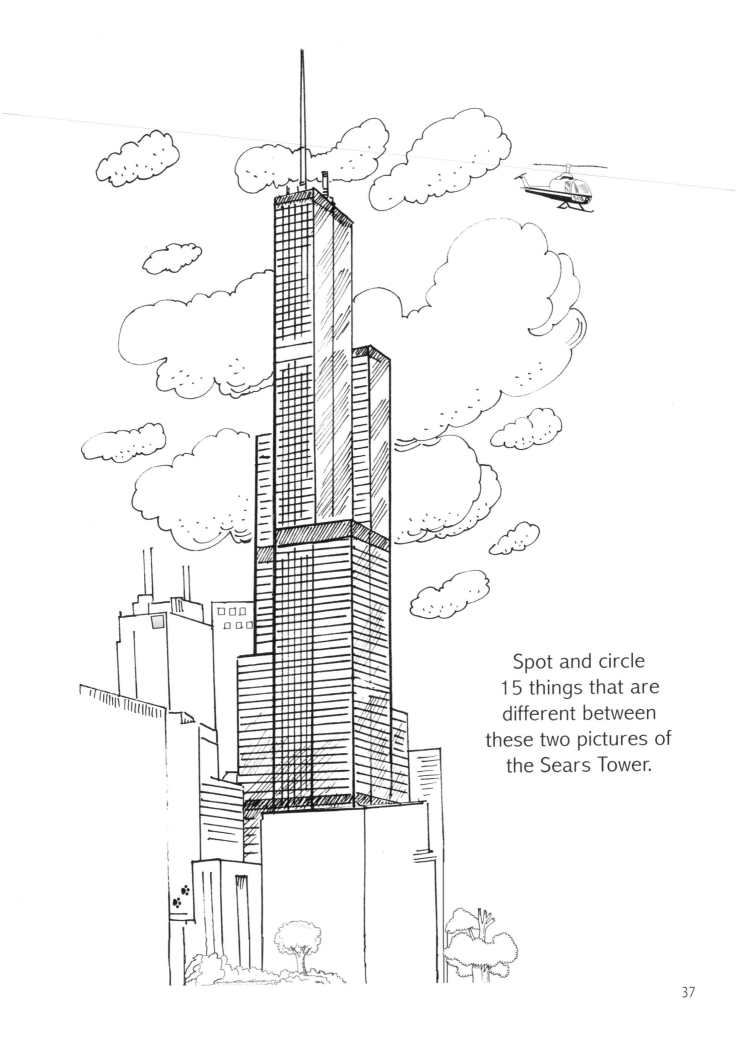

Spot and circle
15 things that are
different between
these two pictures of
the Sears Tower.

The Space Needle, in Seattle, Washington, is a major landmark of the Pacific Northwest. Originally built for the 1962 World's Fair, the 605-foot-tall futuristic tower has become a symbol of Seattle.

Spot and circle
15 things that are
different between
these two pictures of
the Space Needle.

Located in New York Harbor, the Statue of Liberty was a gift of international friendship given by the people of France to the United States in 1886.

Spot and circle
15 things that are
different between
these two pictures of
the Statue of Liberty.

The Alamo, now a museum in San Antonio, Texas, was once a mission and fortress compound. The Battle of the Alamo (fought between the Republic of Mexico and the rebel Texan forces) took place here for thirteen days in 1836.

Spot and circle
15 things that are
different between
these two pictures
of the Alamo.

Solutions

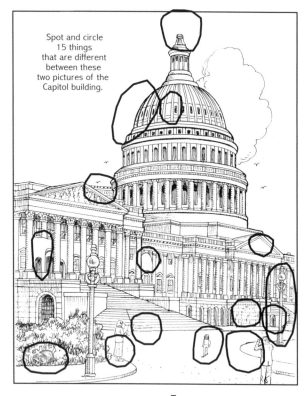

Spot and circle 15 things that are different between these two pictures of the Capitol building.

page 5

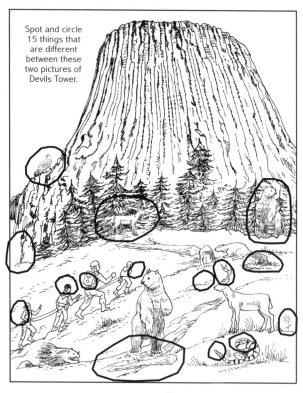

Spot and circle 15 things that are different between these two pictures of Devils Tower.

page 7

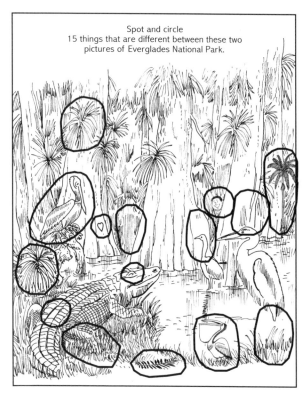

Spot and circle 15 things that are different between these two pictures of Everglades National Park.

page 9

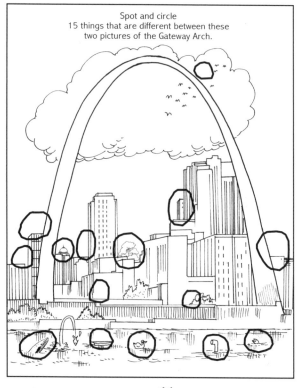

Spot and circle 15 things that are different between these two pictures of the Gateway Arch.

page 11

Spot and circle
15 things that are different
between these two pictures of
the Golden Gate Bridge.

page 13

Spot and circle
15 things that are different between these
two pictures of Graceland.

page 15

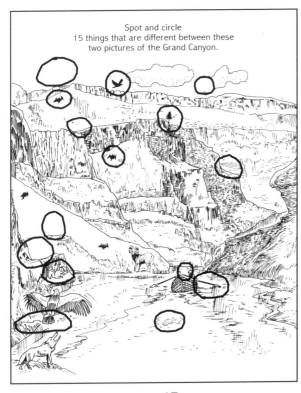

Spot and circle
15 things that are different between these
two pictures of the Grand Canyon.

page 17

Spot and circle
15 things that are different between these
two pictures of the Hollywood Sign.

page 19

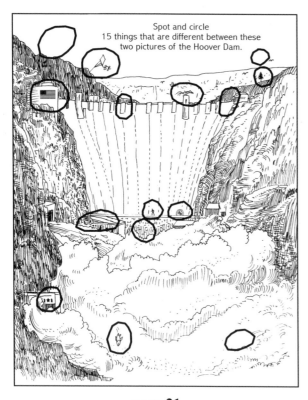

page 21

page 23

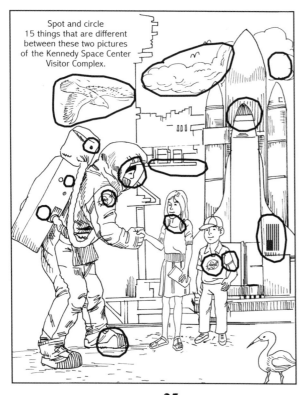

page 25

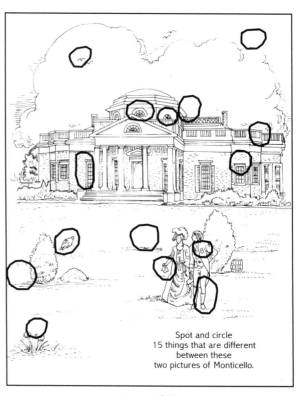

page 27

page 29

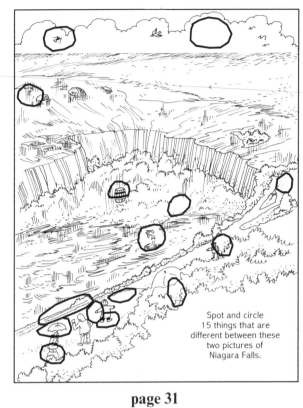

page 31

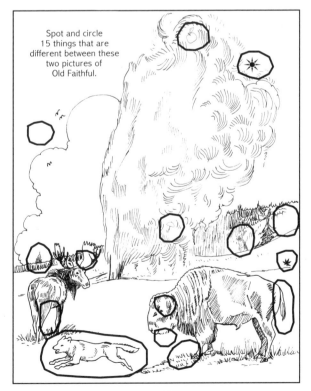

page 33

page 35

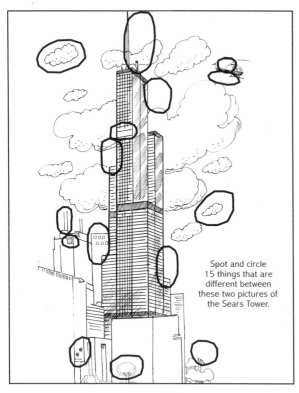

Spot and circle 15 things that are different between these two pictures of the Sears Tower.

page 37

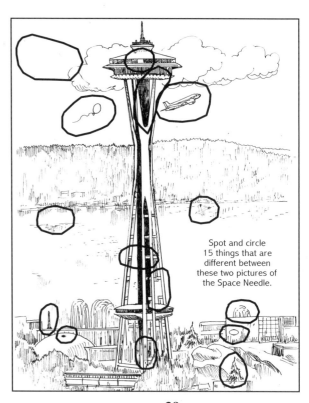

Spot and circle 15 things that are different between these two pictures of the Space Needle.

page 39

Spot and circle 15 things that are different between these two pictures of the Statue of Liberty.

page 41

Spot and circle 15 things that are different between these two pictures of the Alamo.

page 43